WHS

AGE
6–7
Key Stage 1

NATIONAL TESTS
practice papers

FOR THE YEAR **2005**

English
Levels 1–3

practice papers

Contents

Acknowledgements

The Publishers would like to thank the following for permission to reproduce copyright material:

The Sand Horse by Ann Turnbull, illustrated by Michael Foreman, Andersen Press Ltd 1989
Tidy Up, Trevor © Rob Lewis, Random House 1993

Every effort has been made to trace all copyright holders, but if any have been inadvertently overlooked, the Publishers will be pleased to make the necessary arrangements at the first opportunity.

First published in 2005
exclusively for WHSmith by
Hodder Murray,
a member of the Hodder Headline Group
338 Euston Road
London NW1 3BH

Authors: Christine Moorcroft and Ray Barker
Series editor: Louis Fidge
Illustrations: Willie Ryan

Impression 5 4 3 2 1
Year 2006 2005

Printed and bound in Spain

A catalogue record for this title is available from the British Library

ISBN 0 340 88848 2

NOTE: The tests, questions and advice in this book are not reproductions of the official test materials sent to schools. The official testing process is supported by guidance and training for teachers in setting and marking tests and interpreting the results. The results achieved in the tests in this book may not be the same as those achieved in the official tests.

The National Tests: A Summary

What are the National Tests?

Children who attend state schools in England sit National Tests (also known as SATs) at the ages of 7, 11 and 14. Those at ages 11 and 14 are taken at the beginning of May. Those at age 7 can be carried out at any point during the year, as chosen by the teacher. Children in Wales may take the same tests at 11 and 14. All children may also sit optional tests in the intervening years – many schools have chosen to adopt these tests.

The results are used by the school to assess each child's level of knowledge and progress in English and Maths at Key Stage 1 and English, Maths and Science at Key Stages 2 and 3. They also provide useful guidance for the child's next teacher when he or she is planning the year's work.

The educational calendar for children aged 5–14 is structured as follows:

Key Stage	Year	Age by end of year	National Test
1 (KS1)	1	6	
	2	7	KEY STAGE 1
2 (KS2)	3	8	Optional Year 3
	4	9	Optional Year 4
	5	10	Optional Year 5
	6	11	KEY STAGE 2
3 (KS3)	7	12	Optional Year 7
	8	13	Optional Year 8
	9	14	KEY STAGE 3

Timetable

The Key Stage 1 National Tests have so far been carried out in May but, from the school year beginning September 2004, teachers will be allowed greater flexibility as to when they test the children and which tests or tasks they use. Key Stage 1 tests are now based on teacher assessment and can take place at any point during the year as chosen by the teacher.

Key Stage 2 tests take place in one week in May. All children sit the same test at the same time. In 2005, the tests will take place in the week of **9–13 May**. Your child's school will be able to provide you with a detailed timetable.

Key Stage 3 students will sit their tests on **3–6 May 2005**.

Levels

National average levels have been set for children's results in the National Tests. The levels are as follows:

LEVEL	AGE 7 (Key Stage 1)	AGE 11 (Key Stage 2)	AGE 14 (Key Stage 3)
8			
7			
6			
5			
4			
3			
2 2a 2b 2c			
1			

BELOW EXPECTED LEVEL

EXPECTED LEVEL

ABOVE EXPECTED LEVEL

EXCEPTIONAL

Results

Your child's teacher will use the test results and own teacher assessment to decide the level your child is working at and will send you a report indicating this level.

The school's overall test results will be included in local and national league tables, which are published in most newspapers.

What can parents do to help?

While it is never a good idea to encourage cramming, you can help your child to succeed by:

- making sure he or she has enough food, sleep and leisure time during the test period;
- practising important skills such as writing and reading stories, spelling and mental maths;
- telling him or her what to expect in the test, such as important symbols and key words;
- helping him or her to be comfortable in test conditions, including working within a time limit, reading questions carefully and understanding different ways of answering.

How to Use this Book

During Year 2 of Key Stage 1, when your child is seven years old (or will be seven by the end of the following August) he or she will be given a Reading Task and Test. Schools can now choose when to test the children and have a choice of tests to use. Teachers will use the results of these tests to inform their overall assessment of a child's progress.

The purposes of this book

- To prepare children for National Tests in English by giving them practice, so that they will be familiar with the form of the tests they will take.
- To help you to judge your child's progress in English.
- To provide Reading Tests at Level 2 and Level 3 and a Spelling Test at Levels 1 to 3.

The practice tests

- This book includes practice tests on Reading (Levels 2 and 3) and Spelling (Levels 1 to 3).
- Answers and a marking scheme are provided at the end of the book.
- General instructions for all the tests are given below.
- Specific instructions for each test are given in the introduction to that particular test.

Reading Tests (Levels 2 and 3)

- Two separate tests are provided: one for Level 2 and one for Level 3.
- Within each test are two sections: fiction and non-fiction.
- If you are not sure which level of test your child should practise, begin with the Level 2 test. After marking it, look at the marking scheme on page 43. If your child has scored 20 marks or more (the Level 2a range), he or she could try the Level 3 test. If no marks are scored in that range, do not worry: most children reach Level 2 at the *end* of Year 2.

Spelling Test

- All children who do the National Tests take a spelling test. The practice test in this book is similar to this test.

Setting the Tests

- A relaxed approach is best. If you feel anxious, your child will sense this and might not concentrate or perform as well as he or she could.
- Work in a quiet place where you and your child will not be distracted.
- Your child will need a pencil and, if possible, an eraser; if you do not have an eraser, ask your child to cross out any mistakes made.
- No extra paper is needed: your child writes in this book.
- Do not ask your child to do all the tests one after the other.
- Encourage your child and give praise for what he or she can do.
- Do not dwell on what he or she cannot do but, at another time, you could provide practice in the areas where it is needed.
- Be guided by your child's teacher as to what are the best ways in which you can help at home.

Setting the Reading Test: Level 2

Introduction

- This tests up to Level 2, but if your child attains Level 2a, he or she could also try the Level 3 test (page 20).
- There are two parts to the Reading Test: one based on a fiction text (*Tidy Up, Trevor*) and the other on a non-fiction text (*Toys*).
- In the Reading Test, handwriting and spelling do not count, but your child should still try to spell the words as well as possible and to write neatly.
- It is best to give your child a break between the two parts.
- There is no time limit, but the test is unlikely to take more than 45 minutes overall.

Doing the tests – step by step

1 Ask your child to turn to the Fiction Test (page 5). Explain to your child that he or she has to write the answers in this book when doing the test.

2 Read the first page of the story aloud to your child, followed by practice question A. Discuss the four possible answers with your child and ensure that he or she understands why "played tennis" is the correct answer. (In the National Tests, teachers do this to ensure that the children know how to answer the questions and to help them to settle into the test.)

3 Give your child the opportunity to answer practice question B without help, but you can talk about it and help your child to answer it if necessary. The correct answer is "Wednesday". Ensure that your child understands why this is the correct answer.

4 Point out that there are two different types of questions: those which give a choice of answers (one of which your child should tick) and those which ask for a written answer. Written answers need not be complete sentences.

5 Do not help your child to read the rest of the text. You may help with the spelling of the answers. Encourage your child to take care, but point out that he or she may rub out or alter any mistakes made.

6 Ask your child to read one page at a time and then to answer the questions on that page. Tell him or her:

- to find the answers in the text, rather than giving answers which he or she already knows;
- to tick only one box to answer each question;
- that in the Fiction Test the answers are in the text on the same page as the questions;
- to try to answer every question;
- to leave any questions he or she cannot answer, and go back to them at the end;
- to re-read the text to find the answers to any questions which he or she has not answered.

7 Allow your child to read the rest of the text independently and to answer the questions without any help.

8 You may remind your child what to do whenever necessary: for example, to read a page and then answer the questions before turning the page, and to correct mistakes.

9 Repeat the above for the Non-fiction Test (page 15). In this test the questions refer to text on the same page or, if there is no text on the questions page, to the text on the facing page. Your child will not have to turn the page to find the answers.

10 When your child has finished, mark the test paper. The answers and National Curriculum Levels are on page 43.

Level 2 Fiction Test

TIDY UP, TREVOR

Rob Lewis

Trevor was bored.

On Monday he'd done a puzzle.

On Tuesday he'd been roller skating.

On Wednesday he'd painted pictures.

On Thursday he'd played tennis.

Now Trevor didn't know what to do. In the end, he did nothing.

Practice

A What did Trevor do on Thursday?

- ☐ a puzzle
- ☐ went roller skating
- ☐ played tennis
- ☐ nothing

Practice

B On which day did Trevor paint pictures?

____

"Do some digging and weeding," said his dad.

"Play with me," begged his sister.

"Read a book," said his mum.

"Just enjoy yourself, dear," smiled his granny.

1 Who said "Play with me"?

______________________________ 1

2 Who told Trevor just to enjoy himself? 1

- [ ] his sister
- [ ] his dad
- [ ] his mum
- [ ] his granny

TOTAL

2

By lunchtime Trevor was still bored. He was bored and grumpy.

Dad was making sandwiches. "Trevor will help," said Mum.

"You're not doing anything, are you, Trevor?"

"I know just the thing," said Dad. "A trip down the river will cheer you up."

Trevor didn't want to go on a trip down the river.

By now, Mum was fed up too. "If you're not coming with us," she said, "you can go and tidy your cupboard."

3 How did Trevor feel? ✓

☐	excited and happy	☐	tired and happy
☐	bored and grumpy	☐	angry and bad-tempered

1

4 What did Trevor's mum say he could do if he didn't go on the trip down the river?

____

____

1

TOTAL

2

Trevor wished he had gone on the trip down the river.

He flumped down on the floor.

The cupboard door swung open. There were mountains of toys crammed inside. Trevor tugged at a box. Bump! Out fell a very bouncy ball, a bag of feathers, a game of Dingy Dungeons, three jigsaws and a hard, brown lump of Plasticine. It would take him a while to tidy up.

Trevor picked up the very bouncy ball. "I wondered where that was," he said to himself.

5 What did Trevor pick up?

- [ ] a hard, brown lump of Plasticine
- [ ] a very bouncy ball
- [ ] three jigsaws
- [ ] a game of Dingy Dungeons

1

6 What game fell out of the cupboard?

____

1

TOTAL

2

The trip down the river wasn't much fun. No one could forget about Trevor.

"I hope he's all right," said Mum.

Trevor had found some knotty knitting and a crumpled kite.

7 What did Trevor's mum say?

1

8 What two things had Trevor found?

1

TOTAL

2

The river curved under deep green leaves. "I hope Trevor's being good," said Dad.

Trevor had found his blue boat and a rubber ring.

It was time to go home. "I wonder if Trevor has tidied his cupboard," said his sister.

Trevor had found his train set and racing cars.

9 What curved under deep green leaves?

- [ ] a blue boat
- [ ] a rubber ring
- [ ] a train set
- [ ] the river

1

10 What had Trevor found apart from his train set, racing cars and rubber ring?

____

1

TOTAL

2

Back in the garden, Granny was snoring.

"Has Trevor been good?" asked Dad.

"Oh yes," yawned Granny, "as quiet as a mouse."

"Trevor, we're home!" called Mum.

There was no answer.

11 Who had been looking after Trevor?

- [ ] his dad
- [ ] his mum
- [ ] his granny
- [ ] nobody

1

12 Which word tells you that Granny was asleep?

____

1

TOTAL

2

"Trevor, what's all this mess?" Mum shouted.

There was still no answer.

The cupboard was tidy.

"Guess what, Mum," said Trevor.

"I'm not bored any more.

Can I tidy up again tomorrow?"

13 What did Trevor want to do the next day? 1

- [ ] tidy up again
- [ ] go to the river
- [ ] play with his sister
- [ ] nothing

14 Was Trevor still bored? 1

____

TOTAL 2

Level 2 Non-fiction Test

Toys

Introduction

You probably have many different kinds of toys: cuddly toys, indoor games, outdoor games, computer games, toys which move, musical toys, floating toys, things to make and other kinds of toys.

outdoor games

things to make

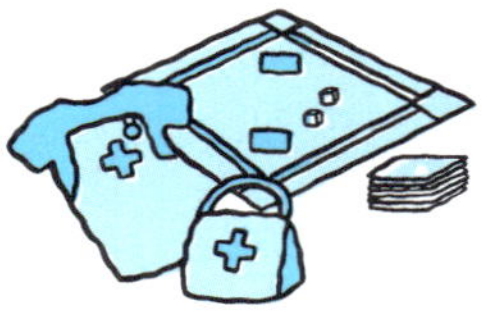

indoor games

musical toys

A What kind of toy is a drum?

- ☐ outdoor game
- ☐ indoor game
- ☐ musical toy
- ☐ something to make

Practice

B Name something used in an outdoor game.

____

Practice

Toys which move

Some toys can move. They cannot move by themselves. Something has to make them move. That something is called a force.

A force can be a push or a pull.

The push or pull can come from a person or something else.

What pushes or pulls toys?			
people	**magnet**	**clockwork**	**battery**
doll's pram	magnetic football	clockwork frog	train
bike	magnetic fishing	clockwork car	racing car
pull-along dog		clockwork police car	

The wind can push or pull some toys: kites, balloons and sail boats.

Some toys move when they go downhill (but you have to take them uphill first!).

15 Which of these toys is moved by batteries? ✓

- [ ] a kite
- [ ] a bike
- [ ] a doll's pram
- [ ] a train

1

16 From where does the push or pull come to move a kite?

____

1

17 A push or a pull is a ✓

- [ ] toy
- [ ] force
- [ ] magnet
- [ ] battery

1

18 What must you do if you want a toy to move downhill?

____

____

1

TOTAL

4

Musical toys

You can make a noise with some toys. You can play a tune with some of them: for example, a mouth-organ, a xylophone and a drum.

There are different ways of making a noise.

You can tap or bang: a drum and a tambourine.

You can shake: a tambourine, a rattle and maracas.

You can pluck: a guitar and a zither.

You can blow: a trumpet, a melodica and a whistle.

A kazoo is blown in the same way as a comb and tissue paper, as if you are saying "aaaah"!

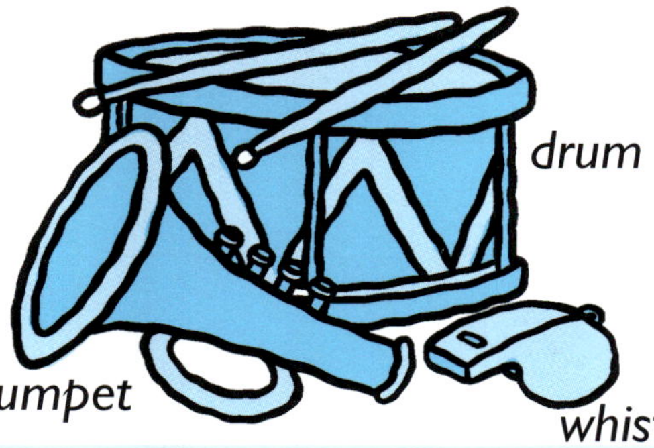

19 Which toy can be shaken or tapped or banged to make a sound?

- ☐ drum
- ☐ xylophone
- ☐ tambourine
- ☐ maracas

1

20 What could you use instead of a kazoo?

____

____

2

TOTAL

3

Floating toys

Some toys float. Inflatables and plastic ducks float. They are full of air and so they are light for their size. They float because they are lighter for their size than water. If water gets in, it pushes out the air and the toy sinks. A sponge floats until it gets waterlogged, and then it sinks.

A model boat made of solid metal will not float. A model boat made of solid wood *will* float. Metal is heavier for its size than water. Most wood is lighter for its size than water.

You can make things float by changing their shape.
A solid ball of Plasticine sinks.
You can flatten the Plasticine; then it will float.

21 Which one of these toys floats?

- [ ] a solid metal boat
- [ ] a boat made of solid wood
- [ ] a solid ball of Plasticine
- [ ] a waterlogged sponge

1

22 What can you do to a ball of Plasticine to make it float?

____

1

23 What makes inflatables float?

____

1

24 Which solid material floats?

____

1

TOTAL

4

Setting the Reading Test: Level 3

Introduction

- There are two parts to this test: one based on a fiction text (*The Sand Horse*) and the other on a non-fiction text (*Animals on the Beach*).
- In the Reading Test, handwriting and spelling do not count, but your child should still try to spell the words as well as possible and to write neatly.
- It is best to give your child a break between the two tests.
- There is no time limit, but the test is unlikely to take more than 45 minutes overall.

If you wish, cut out pages 21 to 31 and staple them together to make a reading booklet.

1 Ask your child to turn to the Fiction Test (page 21). Explain to your child that he or she has to write the answers in this book when doing the test (pages 33–36).

2 Read the first page of the story aloud to your child, followed by practice question A (page 33). Discuss the four possible answers with your child and ensure that he or she understands why "by the sea" is the correct answer. (In the National Tests, teachers do this to ensure that the children know how to answer the questions and to help them to settle into the test.)

3 Give your child the opportunity to answer practice question B without help, but you can talk about it and help your child to answer it if necessary. The correct answer is "the white tops of the waves" or "white crests on the waves" or a similar answer. Ensure that your child understands why that is the correct answer.

4 Point out that there are two different types of questions: those which give a choice of answers (one of which your child should tick) and those which ask for a written answer. Written answers need not be complete sentences.

5 Point out the page numbers in blue above the questions. Explain that these are the pages to look at to find the answers to the questions.

6 Do not help your child to read the rest of the text. You may help with the spelling of the answers. Encourage your child to take care, but point out that he or she may rub out or alter any mistakes made.

7 Ask your child to read one page at a time and then to answer the questions about that page. Tell him or her:

- to find the answers in the text, rather than giving answers which he or she already knows;
- to tick only one box to answer each question;
- to try to answer every question;
- to leave any questions he or she cannot answer, and go back to them at the end;
- to re-read the text to find the answers to any questions which he or she has not answered.

8 Allow your child to read the rest of the text independently and to answer the questions without any help.

9 You may remind your child of what to do whenever necessary: for example, to read a page and then answer the questions before turning the page, and to correct mistakes.

10 Before beginning the Non-fiction Test (page 27), explain to your child that it should be answered in the same way as the Fiction Test. Repeat any of the above steps if necessary. The answers and National Curriculum Levels are on page 44.

Level 3 Reading Test: Fiction

THE SAND HORSE

Story by Ann Turnbull

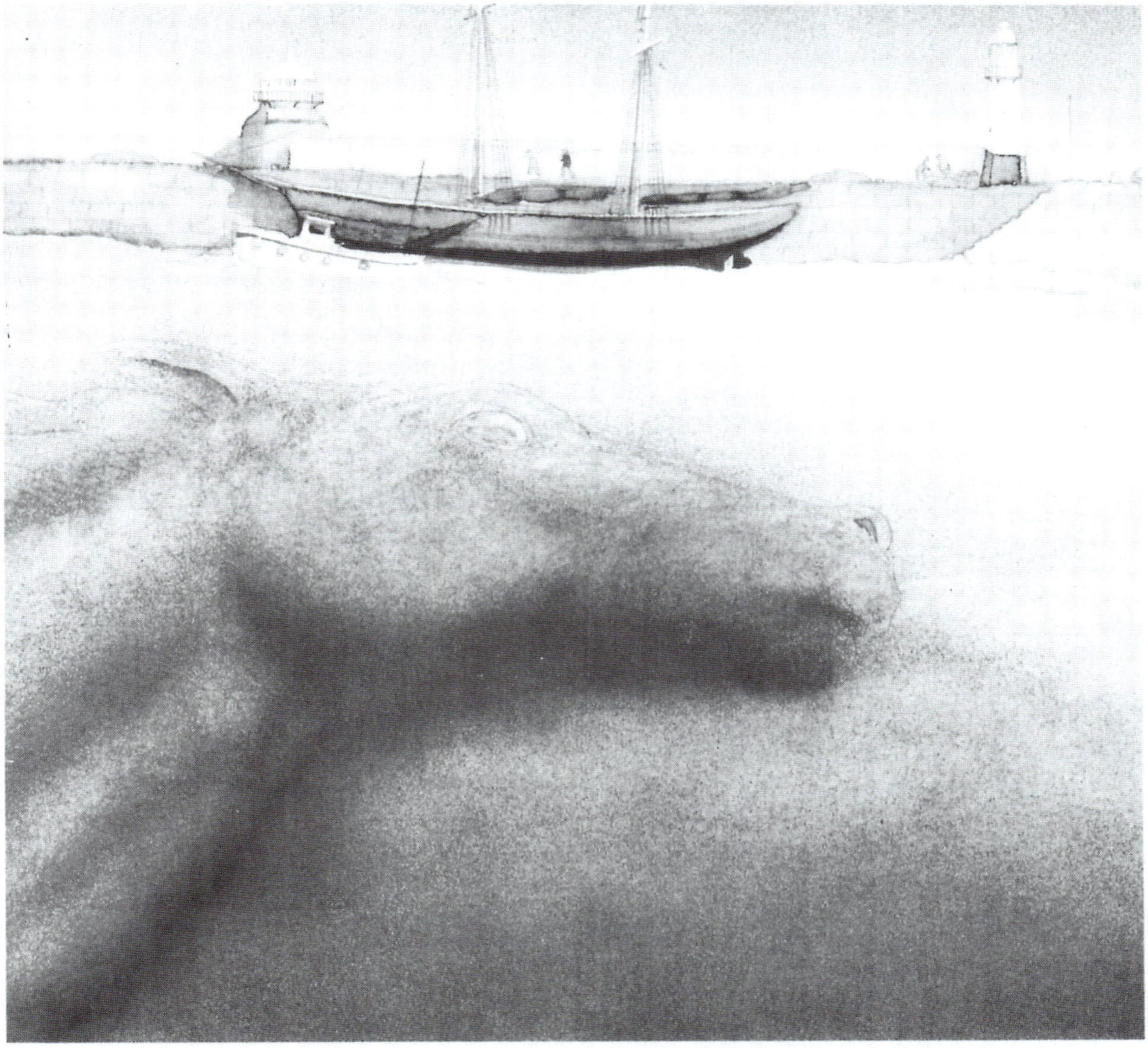

Illustrated by Michael Foreman

Once there was an artist who lived in St Ives. He lived with his wife and baby in a house by the sea. Sometimes the artist worked in his studio, but on fine days in summer he went to the beach and made animals in the sand. He could make dogs and cats and seals and dolphins, but mostly he made horses, because horses, he said, were the most beautiful animals of all.

One morning the artist woke to a brisk blue day with a choppy sea and white crests on the waves.

"Look! White horses!" he said to his wife.

When the sea is rough and the waves have white tops people call them white horses.

The artist saw them: far out in the bay, plunging and galloping, tossing spray from their manes.

"Today I shall make a horse," he said.

He went to the beach. He marked out his pitch, put his hat down on the sand, and started work.

First he fetched water from the sea. He splashed some on to the dry sand. He patted and moulded the sand.

The horse began to appear: muscles and hooves, raised head and rippling mane.

The beach filled up with people. They stopped and admired the sand horse. They threw money, and the coins clinked in the artist's hat.

The horse grew. He was a galloping horse, galloping forever on his side.

All day the artist worked on his horse, shaping the muscles of his legs and neck, twisting each curl of his mane.

He worked until the sun set and the beach grew cold. Families began leaving. They folded their deck-chairs and shook sand from their clothes.

The artist scooped up the coins in his hat and went home.

The sand horse woke up.

He was alive, but he could not move. He opened one eye, but all he saw were clouds.

He listened with his one ear. He heard seagulls. He heard the boom and hiss of the sea. And faintly, in the crash of waves, he heard neighing.

A seagull landed on his back, and walked about, jabbing the air with his sharp beak.

"Seagull," said the sand horse, "what's that neighing I hear?"

"That's the white horses," said the seagull, "out in the bay."

"What are they doing?"

"They are prancing and frisking and flicking their tails."

"Where are they going?"

"Everywhere!" said the seagull. "Newlyn, Polperro, Mevagissey, Marazion –"

"I want to go with them!" cried the sand horse.

"You!" The seagull wheeled up in the air, laughing, and all his friends joined in. He swooped down again and said, "You! You are only a sand horse. You can't go with them."

The sand horse tried to move. He was a galloping horse, but he was fixed in the sand. He could not go with them.

The sky darkened. The seagulls flew away. The boom of the sea was louder.

Much closer now, the sand horse heard the white horses neighing.

"Come with us!" they called.

The sea crashed on the shore, flinging spray over the sand horse.

"Come with us!"

The sea crashed again, and the sand horse was soaked with spray.

"Come with us!" called the white horses. "To Sennen, Land's End, and the Longships Light!"

A wave broke and flooded the sand horse, drenching his head and mane.

"I'm coming!" he called. "Wait for me!"

Another wave broke, and the sea was foaming all around the outline of the sand horse, filling every space. The sea sucked and pulled. It was pulling him down the beach.

"I'm coming! I'm coming!" he cried.

A huge wave rolled up the beach. It reared, curled over, and smashed down upon the sand horse, washing away his mane, his head, his legs, and his body. It went hissing back down to the sea, dragging the sand horse with it.

The sand horse felt waves buoying him up. Amongst the waves white horses were prancing. He neighed and tossed his mane.

His hooves struck spray from the sea.

"I can move!" he cried. "I can gallop!"

He frisked and galloped. He swished his white tail.

All around him the white horses plunged and jumped the waves.

"To Sennen!" they neighed. "To Land's End and the Lizard!"

They galloped away, and the sand horse went with them.

Next morning, when the artist came down to the beach, people looked at the smooth sand and said, "It's a shame. All that work washed away."

But the artist smiled.

He knew where his sand horse had gone.

Level 3 Reading Test: Non-fiction

Animals on the Beach

The story of *The Sand Horse* is set in Cornwall, in the south of England. Cornwall has many beaches.

The next four pages are about some of the animals found on beaches. These animals are found on beaches because beaches have everything they need. Some of them need to live in salt water, others eat the plants which grow on beaches and some eat other animals which live in sand or salt water.

Animals with shells

Shells are the skeletons of sea creatures called molluscs – animals with soft bodies and no bones inside them.

Some molluscs live on the shore. Others live in the sea. The shells of dead molluscs are sometimes washed up on to the beach.

Some molluscs have one shell. These molluscs are called gastropods. Whelks, cowries, limpets and periwinkles are gastropods.

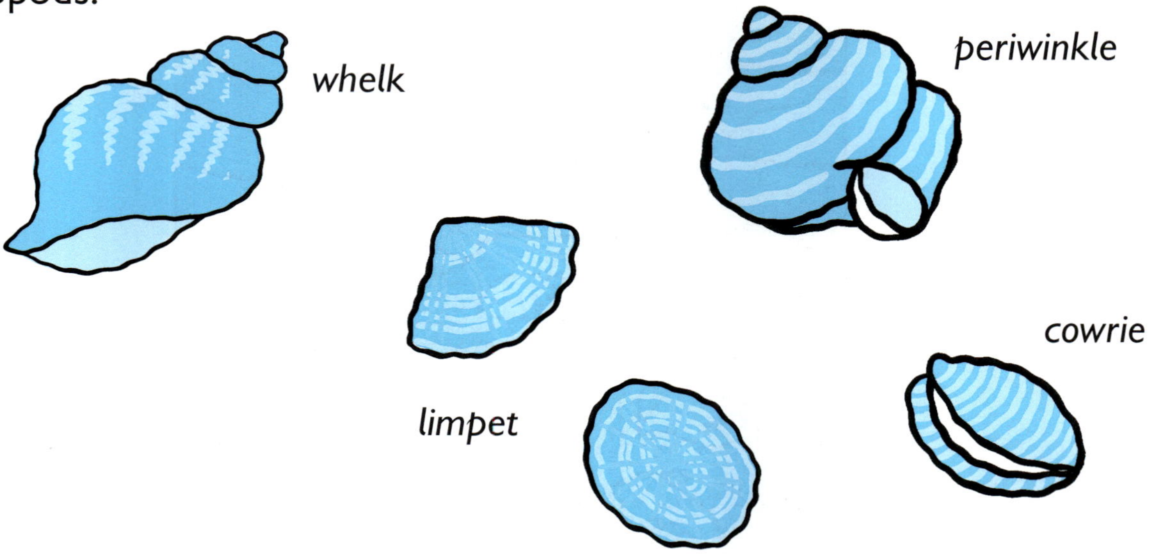

Some gastropods eat seaweed. They scrape the plant with their rough tongue. Some gastropods eat other molluscs. Their sharp tongue can drill a hole in a shell. They use their tongue to scrape out the animal inside.

Some molluscs have two shells joined like a hinge. These molluscs are called bivalves.

Mussels, scallops and cockles are bivalves. Mussels make thin brown threads which they use to fix themselves on to rocks. The sea washes over them but they stay fixed to the rocks.

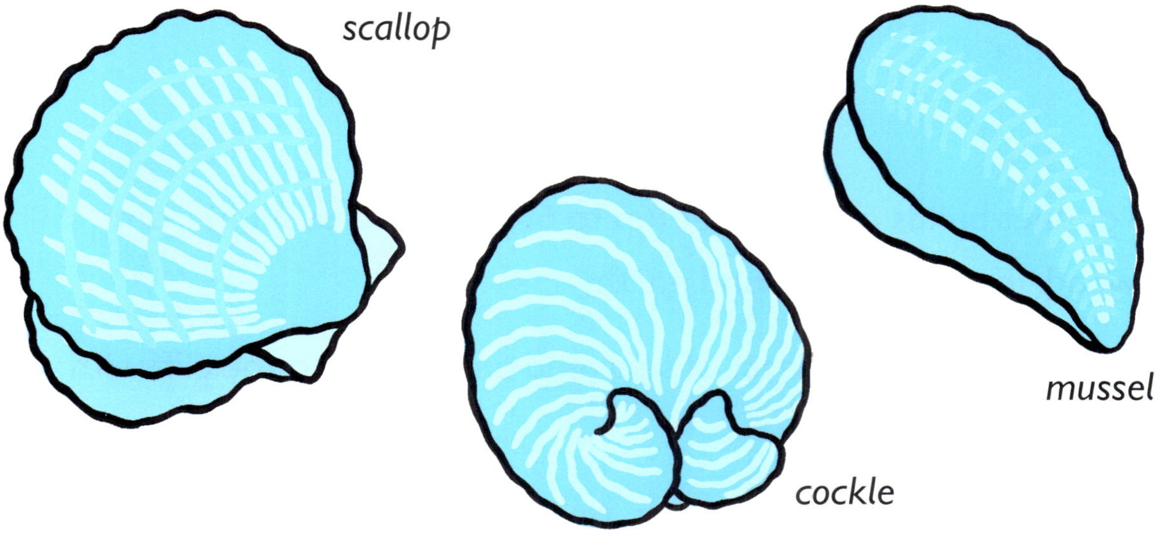

Cockles have ribbed shells which help them to grip the sand where they live. They eat bits of small dead plants and animals which they suck from the sand through a tube.

Barnacles are not molluscs but they look rather like them. They build a hard wall around their body, which looks a bit like a shell. Barnacles cling to rocks on the shore. They also cling to the bottoms of boats and ships.

The hermit crab has no shell. It finds an empty shell and creeps inside it. The shell has to be just the right size for the hermit crab's body. As the hermit crab grows it has to find a bigger shell.

Birds

Some birds nest on cliffs near the sea. The puffin nests in soft parts of the cliff, where it can burrow with its large bill.

puffin

The gannet builds a large nest (up to 60 centimetres high) from seaweed, feathers, grass and earth.

The kittiwake makes a nest of seaweed and fixes it to the cliff with mud.

The herring gull nests in colonies, on the ground and on ledges on cliffs. It even nests on the ledges of buildings. The razorbill also nests in colonies. It does not build a nest, but lays one egg in a crack or under a rock on the cliff.

The guillemot lays one egg. It does not build a nest, but lays its egg on the bare rock. The egg is pear-shaped, so it rolls around but does not roll off the cliff.

guillemot

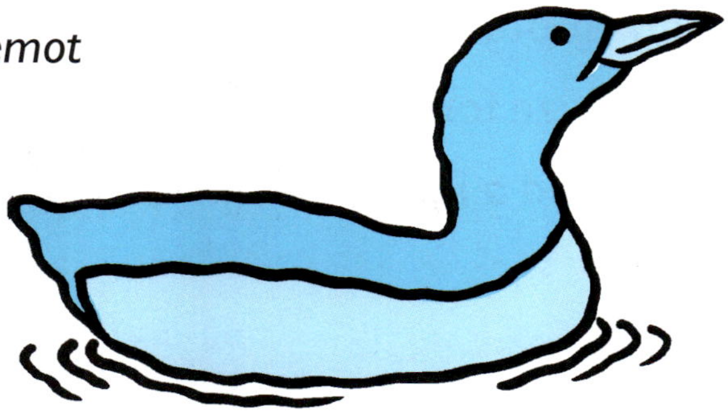

razorbill

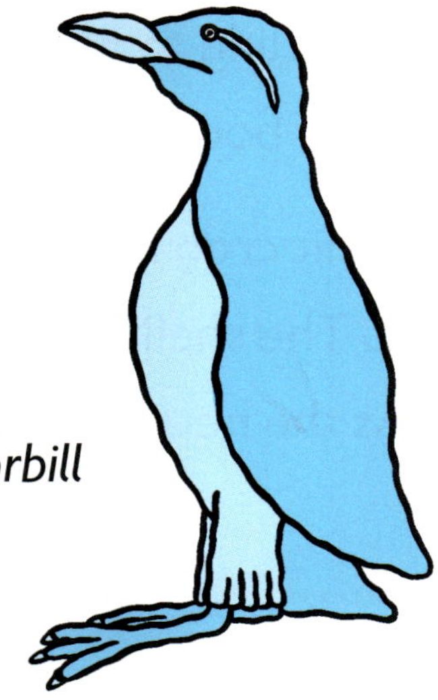

Animals in rock pools

When the tide goes out, some animals stay in rock pools; some of them fix themselves to the rocks.

dahlia anemone

Sea anemones have the name of a flower but they are animals.

The dahlia anemone has bright blue, pink and white tentacles. It sticks bits of shell and gravel to its tentacles to make it hard to see.

The beadlet anemone has pink tentacles. It waves them about to catch shrimps or small fish to eat. When it catches one it stings the animal with one tentacle and then uses the others to push it into its mouth.

beadlet anemone

Most starfish have five arms, like a star, but the common sunstar can have up to thirteen arms. The starfish has rows of suckers along its arms. It uses them to pull itself along.

starfish

You might find small fish in rock pools, like the blenny and the goby. They look alike, but the fins on their backs are different. The goby has two but the blenny has one.

End of Level 3 Reading Booklet

Fiction Test Questions on:

The Sand Horse

A Where was the artist's house? PAGE 22

- [ ] in a wood
- [ ] by the sea
- [ ] in a field
- [ ] by a river

Practice

B What were the "white horses" on the sea?

____

Practice

PAGES 23 AND 24

1 Why did the sand horse gallop on his side?

1

---

2 What could the sand horse hear out in the bay?

1

- [ ] coins clinking
- [ ] people
- [ ] another sand horse
- [ ] white horses neighing

3 What landed on the sand horse's back?

1

- [ ] a big wave
- [ ] a seagull
- [ ] a stone
- [ ] sand

4 What did the sand horse want to do?

1

TOTAL

4

PAGES 24 AND 25

5 How can you tell that the seagull thought the sand horse was silly?

1

6 Why couldn't the sand horse go with the white horses?

1

7 How can you tell that night was falling?

- [ ] the moon was shining
- [ ] the sea crashed on the shore
- [ ] the sky darkened
- [ ] the stars twinkled

1

8 Which word tells you that the sea was powerful?

- [ ] spray
- [ ] soaked
- [ ] flooded
- [ ] crashed

1

TOTAL

4

PAGE 26

1

9 Which words make you think that the sand horse was being damaged by the sea?

1

10 Which words tell you that the sand horse was floating?

1

11 What made the artist happy? ✓

☐ he knew where his sand horse had gone	☐ people had put money in his hat
☐ he was going to make another sand horse	☐ he found a lizard

TOTAL

3

Non-fiction Test Questions on:

Animals on the Beach

PAGES 27, 28 AND 29

12 Where is Cornwall? 1

13 What are shells? 1

- [ ] skeletons of sea creatures
- [ ] plants
- [ ] stones
- [ ] animals

14 Name a mollusc that has one shell. 1

15 How many shells do bivalves have? 1

- [ ] one
- [ ] six
- [ ] two
- [ ] none

TOTAL 4

PAGES 29 AND 30

16 Barnacles cling to rocks. What else do they cling to?

2

17 A cockle grips the sand

- [ ] with thin brown threads
- [ ] with a tube
- [ ] with its ribbed shell
- [ ] with suckers

1

18 Name two sea birds which lay just one egg.

2

19 Which bird lays a pear-shaped egg?

- [ ] herring gull
- [ ] gannet
- [ ] puffin
- [ ] guillemot

1

TOTAL

6

PAGES 30 AND 31

20 Where does the puffin nest?

____

Why?

____

2

21 Beadlet and dahlia are types of ✓

- [ ] crab
- [ ] gastropod
- [ ] starfish
- [ ] sea anemone

1

22 Which is a word for feelers? ✓

- [ ] tentacles
- [ ] suckers
- [ ] ledge
- [ ] wedged

1

TOTAL

4

Setting the Spelling Test

- The Spelling Test is in two parts: a picture test and a text test.
- There is no time limit, but it should not take more than 30 minutes to complete both parts of the test.

Spelling Picture Test

1 Explain to your child that he or she has to write the answers on page 41.

2 With your child, talk about what can be seen in the pictures.

3 Make sure he or she knows the word for what is shown in each of the pictures (look at the answers on page 45).

4 Ask your child to write in the box beneath each small picture the word for what is shown. If necessary, remind him or her what the pictures show.

5 When your child has finished, mark the test using the marking scheme on page 45.

Spelling Text Test

1 Copy the complete text on page 45 on to a separate piece of paper. Underline the words in bold type – these are the missing words.

2 Ask your child to listen to you reading the complete text.

3 Ask your child to look at his or her copy of the text (page 42). Point out that some of the words have been left out. Give your child the opportunity to guess the first missing word, as practice. The correct answer is "the". Ensure he or she writes the word correctly in the space provided, and that he or she understands the task.

4 Tell your child that you are going to read the text again and that he or she should write in the missing words as you read.

5 Read the text aloud again, pausing after each missing word, to give your child time to write it on the test copy. You can repeat each of the missing words up to three times, if necessary.

6 Mark the answers, using the marking scheme on page 46.

Spelling Picture Test

The Carnival

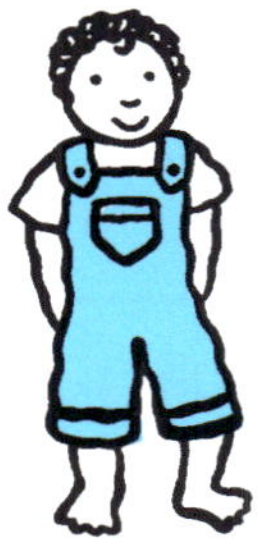

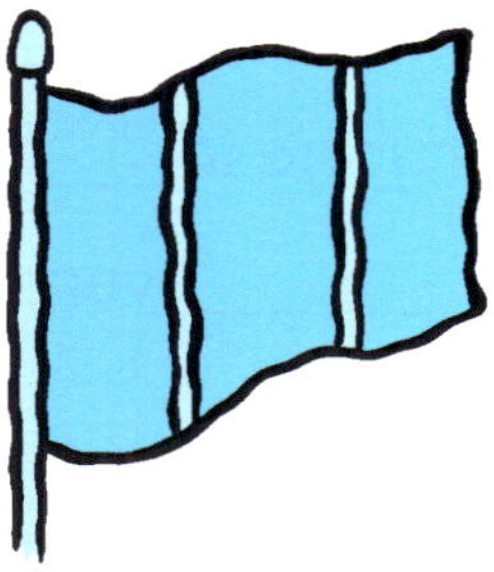

TOTAL

20

Spelling Text Test
The Carnival

Everyone in __________ town was preparing for the carnival. __________ were decorating __________ and __________ things to wear.

The children at Tom and Jackie's __________ were __________ to dress up as __________. Tom __________ his mum if he could wear her __________ scarf on his __________. She made a __________ for him to wear __________ one __________. All he needed was a __________ parrot to sit on his shoulder.

Jackie had a __________, curved sword made of __________. Her grandad had made a hat for her. It was __________ with a skull and two crossed white bones on it.

__________ it was the __________ of carnival day. The children couldn't wait to __________ their __________.

TOTAL

40

Answers

Reading Test: Level 2

Level 2 Reading Test: Fiction *Tidy Up, Trevor*

Question	Answer	Mark	Question	Answer	Mark
A	Played tennis	_	**7**	I hope he's all right	1
B	Wednesday	_	**8**	Some knotty knitting and a crumpled kite	1
1	Trevor's sister	1	**9**	The river	1
2	His granny	1	**10**	His blue boat	1
3	Bored and grumpy	1	**11**	His granny	1
4	Tidy his cupboard	1	**12**	Snoring	1
5	A very bouncy ball	1	**13**	Tidy up again	1
6	Dingy Dungeons	1	**14**	No	1

Maximum mark: 14

Level 2 Reading Test: Non-fiction *Toys*

Question	Answer	Mark	Question	Answer	Mark
A	Musical toy	_	**19**	Tambourine	1
B	Bat, Ball, Racquet *or* Wickets	_	**20**	A comb and tissue paper	2 if both answers are given
15	A train	1	**21**	A boat made of solid wood	1
16	The wind	1	**22**	Change its shape *or* flatten it	1
17	Force	1	**23**	Air	1
18	Take it uphill	1	**24**	Wood	1

Maximum mark: 11

Maximum mark for Reading Test: Level 2 = 25

National Curriculum Levels

Marks	0–6	7–13	14–19	20–25
National Curriculum Level	Below 2	2c	2b	2a

Answers

Reading Test: Level 3

Level 3 Reading Test: Fiction *The Sand Horse*

Question	Answer	Mark	Question	Answer	Mark
A	By the sea	_	**6**	He could not move/he was fixed in the sand	1
B	The white tops of the waves	_	**7**	The sky darkened	1
1	He had only one side/ He was made lying flat on the sand	1	**8**	Crashed	1
2	White horses neighing	1	**9**	Smashed *or* washing away *or* dragging	1
3	A seagull	1	**10**	Buoying him up	1
4	Go with the white horses	1	**11**	He knew where his sand horse had gone	1
5	He laughed at him	1			

Maximum mark: 11

Level 3 Reading Test: Non-fiction *Animals on the Beach*

Question	Answer	Mark	Question	Answer	Mark
12	In the south of England	1	**18**	Razorbill and guillemot	2 if both answers are given
13	Skeletons of sea creatures	1	**19**	Guillemot	1
14	Whelk, cowrie, limpet *or* periwinkle	1	**20**	In soft parts of the cliff so that it can burrow into it with its bill	2 if both answers are given
15	Two	1	**21**	Sea anemone	1
16	The bottoms of boats and ships	2 if both answers are given	**22**	Tentacles	1
17	With its ribbed shell	1			

Maximum mark: 14

Maximum mark for Reading Test: Level 3 = 25

National Curriculum Levels

Marks	0–13	14–25
National Curriculum Level	Below 3	3

Spelling Test Marking Scheme

Give one mark for getting the initial letter string (initial sound) of a word right and another for the whole word. A total of two marks per word is available.

Spelling Picture Test

Question	Answer	Mark
1	hat	2
2	boy	2
3	flag	2
4	king	2
5	crown	2
6	truck	2
7	fairy	2
8	star	2
9	sweets	2
10	witch	2

Maximum mark: 20

Spelling Text Test

Everyone in **the** town was preparing for the carnival. **People** were decorating **trucks** and **making** things to wear.

The children at Tom and Jackie's **school** were **going** to dress up as **pirates**. Tom **asked** his mum if he could wear her **red** scarf on his **head**. She made a **patch** for him to wear **over** one **eye**. All he needed was a **talking** parrot to sit on his shoulder.

Jackie had a **long**, curved sword made of **cardboard**. Her grandad had made a hat for her. It was **black** with a skull and two crossed white bones on it.

Soon it was the **morning** of carnival day. The children couldn't wait to **join** their **friends**.

See page 46 for guidance in awarding marks.

Answers

Spelling Text Test

Question	Answer	Mark
Practice	the	–
1	people	2
2	trucks	2
3	making	2
4	school	2
5	going	2
6	pirates	2
7	asked	2
8	red	2
9	head	2
10	patch	2
11	over	2
12	eye	2
13	talking	2
14	long	2
15	cardboard	2
16	black	2
17	soon	2
18	morning	2
19	join	2
20	friends	2

Maximum mark: 40

Maximum mark for Spelling Test: 60

National Curriculum Levels

Marks	0–12	13–30	31–47	48–60
National Curriculum Level	Below 1	1	2	3